Options Trading

QuickStart Guide

Knowing The Foreign Exchange Pairs and how to trade them without shrinking your balance

Written By

Zach Raymond

Disclaimer

High Risk Investment

Trading on margin carries a high level of risk and may not be suitable for all investors.

The high degree of leverage can work against you as well as for you. The possibility exists that you could sustain a loss in excess to your investment. Before deciding to trade foreign exchange you should carefully consider your investment objectives, level of experience, and risk appetite.

You should be aware of all the risks associated with foreign exchange trading and seek advice from an independent financial advisor if you have any doubts. Any opinions, news, research, analyses, prices, or other information contained on this book is provided as general market commentary and does not constitute investment advice.

Author will not accept liability for any loss or damage, including without limitation to, any loss of profit, which may arise directly or indirectly from use of or reliance on such information.

Description

When it comes to the world of investing, it really can feel like a jungle out there. There are so many things you are supposed to do, things you aren't supposed to do, and things that you should definitely do if you want to make it big.

There are definitely rules you should follow, and there are little tips and secrets of things you can do that will make your entire process go a lot easier. You know you want to break out of the simplicity of everyday investing and dive into the world of bigger and better stocks, but to do that, you are going to need some help.

That is where this book comes in. In it, you are going to discover the tips and trick of options trading, and how you can use that to make your investing go a lot easier.

Sound confusing?

Don't worry, it isn't. Options trading, just like all the other investments, are relatively easy to accomplish once you get the hang of things. Once you know how to understand what you are supposed to understand, and once you know the key things you are supposed to learn, this is going to feel like a breeze.

Let me show you how you can use options to grow your investments, make the money you want to make, and expand your investing career. You are going to learn all of the little things to keep in mind, the insider tips that will launch you to success, and the things you need to avoid that will hold you back.

Sound exciting?

Good, I knew it would.

- Learn how to handle the little things in options trading

- Learn how to handle the big things

- Discover the keys you need to make your options trading successful

- And more!

Main Contents

Introduction

Welcome to the world of investments.

You feel really important now, you know what the different terms mean, you know how to make good choices that are going to lead to the greatest outcome, and you know how to invest in things that grow your portfolio in the best way possible.

You feel like one of the biggest wolves on Wall Street as you make your decisions on a daily basis. You know that you can make small choices now that affect your small choices later, and you know that these choices are going to end up being big choices one day.

The more you put into it, the better it is, and the more money and experience you get at the end of the day. So, you feel like you have some seasons under your belt, and you are now ready to take things to the next level. You are now ready to step out of the sandbox and onto the playground with the big kids, and you are ready to make those harder choices.

But you feel lost. This is a big world and investments are nothing to fool around with. You know you need to make smart choices, or they are going to fall back on you in ways you don't want to happen, so you have to know what you are doing.

And you don't.

There are so many options out there... how do you know you're making the right choice? There are so many different ways you can do this, how do you know you are being smart about it?

There are so many other things that are tempting to try, how do you know you are making the right decision to gain the greatest results? With these questions and more floating around in your head, how do you know what to do?

And that is where this book comes in. In it, I am going to show you what you need to know with your options trading, what you can do to be successful in it, and how you can get the greatest results out of what you are doing, all in minimal time and with no stress.

So if you are ready to break out of the simple little trades you have been doing, step up to the plate. You are running with the big kids now.

Chapter 1 – What Are Your Options? An Overview

I am sure you have noticed that the world of investing is one that is as elaborate and intricate as the variety of things you can invest in. It seems no matter what you do, you have to know what terms there are, what those terms mean, and what you can do with those terms.

This, in turn, brings on a whole new world of questions, meaning you need a whole new list of terms to learn, with each of those terms having their own meaning. You need to know not only what these mean, but how you can use them to your own benefit, and how you can get the greatest profit from those terms.

But, as with all forms of business, if you want to get the most out of your business, you have to have an understanding of what you are talking about. Which means you have to know what the terms mean up front. This is what we are going to look at in this first chapter.

So let's get started: First of all, what are options?

An option is a contract just like any other investment, only this is a contract that gives the investor more freedom. As you know with most investments, you do have the right to buy and sell, but that right is somewhat restricted when it comes to when you can do the buying and selling.

Options, on the other hand, are exactly what they say they are... or rather, they do what they say they do. They give you the option to buy when you want to buy and sell when you want to sell, all for the prices you want.

However, an option is still binding, and you do have terms and restrictions that apply in your transactions.

For example: You may be able to get an excellent deal by purchasing an item up front, then learning that it is worth a lot more than you paid for it. Then, later on, you are able to sell it at a profit.

The benefit of these is that you can potentially purchase something at a great price and gain more profit from it later on, but the drawback is that you may end up buying something that you later find out is completely worthless.

Think of it this way.

You decide to purchase a car, but you don't have the money for it up front. You put five thousand dollars for it down, and agree to pay the remaining twenty thousand later, but then you discover that the car is actually worth a lot more than the twenty thousand.

So, you come out ahead. You get to pay the twenty thousand and get the car, because that is the amount that was agreed, then you can sell it for what it is really worth.

On the other hand, you may put the five thousand down on the car, but discover that the car is completely worthless. Now, you aren't obligated to then complete the twenty thousand, but you do have to pay the five thousand. This is the drawback to these kinds of investments.

Another important thing to take note of is that there are two kinds of options, and both kinds of options have both buyers and sellers

First you have calls, and you have puts. These are the two kinds of options. Then, you have the buyers of the calls, the sellers of the calls, the buyers of the puts, and the sellers of the puts.

Which means there are four kinds of participants on the market.

These four groups can be divided into two groups, however. The sellers are known as the writers on the market, and the buyers are known as the holders. The holders, or buyers, on the market are said to have long positions, while the writers, or sellers, are said to have short positions.

One of the most important things you can know about the market is that there is a single, primary distinction between the buyers and the sellers on the market.

Buyers are not required to buy or sell. This is both why they have the long term holding position, and why sellers are called short term holders.

Sellers are required to buy or sell. While a buyer doesn't necessarily need to follow up on a purchase, the seller does need to follow up on a promise to sell.

I know this sounds confusing, as a matter of fact, it is confusing. But, the more you practice, the more you will get used to the entire concept, and you will settle in to the entire system.

Just take your time and get used to it. The more you practice, the easier it is going to be, and in no time at all you will be in the swing of things.

Chapter 2 – What's In It For Me? Why You Should Use Options

With all of the other options out there, you may be wondering why you should choose options as your investment of choice. Of course, you have seen that there are great benefits to being the buyer in this kind of situation, but that doesn't necessarily mean that this is the best choice for you.

Let's take a moment now to look at those reasons, and why they are a great thing for you to consider.

One of the biggest advantages of options is that you aren't limited to making a profit only when the market is going up. This gives you the ability to make a profit when the market is going down, or even when it has leveled off

This gives you the ability to keep moving forward with your investments even when the market itself isn't doing so well. This gives you the opportunity to move forward, even when you may not be.

Now, don't get too excited yet, because this is where options can get deceptive. Options have a reputation for being risky, and with good reason. In order to be successful at options, you have to be able to know where the market is going overall.

Like I said, due to the nature of these options, you are going to be able to make money even when the market is plummeting or at a standstill, but on the other hand, you have to know overall which direction the market is going and tag along with that, even if you are using options.

With the riskiness involved, you may be wondering now why people use options, especially knowing the potential to lose money. However, the answer is simple.

When it comes to options, you have to play the game properly, and to do this, you need leverage. The more leverage you have in a stock, the better off you are going to be.

This is what will give you that incredible boost and the maximum amount of profits.

Another one of the pros in favor of options is that you can use them to hedge your investments. This means you can use options as a source of profit for when your other investments are in a season of downturn.

By using options, you are going to be able to give yourself something to fall back on if you need. This is going to allow you to perhaps risk more with your other investments, or to have a greater peace of mind as you make your choices.

Do keep in mind, as I have already said, you have to be careful about the investments you choose, and there is always the chance you are going to lose money on the options you have. While you can use these as a safeguard for your other investments, you can potentially lose money from your other investments on these kinds of stocks.

I highly recommend that you do your research beforehand, and you carefully pick what works for you. If you feel comfortable with the risk, then by all means go with that, but if you are worried about what you could potentially lose, I recommend that you choose your other stocks carefully, and only keep your option investments at a minimum.

I don't want to scare you off from the options, but I don't want you to fall into the trap of thinking that you are going to have a foolproof safety guard when you hear the advice of using options as a safeguard. I recommend you do always have at least one or two on your list, but keep in mind they could potentially cost you money just as much as any other stock.

You can read the tips and tricks of the alleged stock 'experts', but remember that they are also subject to what the particular investor wants.

You are going to hit both ends of the spectrum when it comes to the experts themselves, and while they may swear by something themselves, you may or may not agree with them.

With that said, I still recommend you take a look at what the experts are saying, and that you are aware of the reason behind what they suggest

Now, one good thing to keep in mind is that there are experts that argue if you need to have a hedge on your investments, then you shouldn't invest in them, but there are plenty of others that say if you are going to invest at all, you should have safeguards in place.

Basically, you have to decide how you feel about it, and go with that. There isn't necessarily a wrong way to do this, but you do need to keep all of your facts straight when you begin any new regime.

Remember to explore all of your options, options. While not all companies allow their employees to hold options, a large amount of companies do.

This in itself gives you an easy 'in' in the option world, giving you that boost you need to get started

Many people, and perhaps you are one of these people, hesitate to get involved in these kinds of stocks because you have to work your way up to the top, as with all other stocks.

This can deter even the most excited stock holder or prospective buyer, meaning you may or may not want to even get started.

But, if there were a way for you to jump in and climb to the top, this is a great way to make that happen. If your company allows for employee options, I highly recommend you get on board. You are going to get many of the same benefits that others option holders have, but you are also going to have the opportunity work with the company itself.

As I am sure you have noticed, most of the stock options you have seen are between two individuals. This is because you are able to cover so much more with your options than with other kinds of stocks.

However, if you work with a company, you are going to have more variety in what you can use your options for.

Chapter 3 – Where's The Accent? American Or European Options

I have already pointed out that there are two kinds of options... the calls and the puts, but in addition to these, there are also two types of options... American and European.

As with other stocks, different kinds of options are going to have their different kinds of styles and rules, and these have absolutely nothing to do with the geographical location of the stocks or stock holders.

Before we get into the fine details of the types of options, let's take a look at the difference between the two.

American options are incredibly flexible. You can buy them then sell them whenever you want, no matter what the value is, the market is, or the date is.

These offer the buyer a lot of variety, and can open the door to a lot of profit. As with all options and option trading, however, they do come with their pros and cons.

Most of the exchange traded options are American type options

European options are similar to the American options, but they are different in one key point.

You can buy these options when you want, you can use them as hedges if you like, you can gain a lot of money from them, or you can potentially lose money on them, but the main way they are different is that European options are more restricting than the American options.

While you can purchase one of these options at any time, you have to wait until the European option comes to its full term before you can sell it.

Either one of these options can be used as short term options, which more often than not is what people are looking for. Most people like to buy, sell, trade, and be done with it. But, there are always benefits to going long term with things, and options are no exception.

While many of the options you find are going to be short term, there are a wide selection of long term options that can range anywhere from one year to even decades. While these long term options aren't available for all stocks, you are going to have a nice selection to choose from.

Up until this point, we have talked about a lot of different options, but they all come down to a single term... plain vanilla.

This means they are really straight forward and basic, regardless of whether or not they are long term, short term, American, or European. While there is nothing wrong with this, there is another variety of option that you need to be aware of.

These are the exotic options

Another way to put these common options is that they are standard... but there is also a nonstandard option out there... which is known as an exotic option.

You may wonder what the difference is between these standard options and the exotic options, and the short answer is... not much. Really, the basic difference you are going to run into is the way the payment on them work.

While this is plain and simple in and of itself, there is a catch.

When it comes to the standard options, you are going to run into the most basic kind of payment plan they have. You are going to be able to expect the same result over and over, and you are going to have a pretty good idea of what you can do with each option.

Think of them as rather generic, run of the mill options that have a standard list of things that happen when you use them. Of course there is going to be some variations, and you do have to account for the minor adjustments that come into play with each, but all in all, you will know what to expect.

Exotic options, on the other hand, are a little trickier. There are things that you need to pay attention to, there are things that you need to change from stock to stock, and there are times when you are going to run into special allowances that only apply to that particular stock.

In other words, you are going to run into a whole new list of details that may vary, and you may have to work on learning as you go with a few of the options. I know this can be frustrating and confusing, but trust me, the more you do, the easier it is going to become.

The true key to success in the options world is to learn the lingo, the details, and how to roll with the changes you are going to find.

There are those little cookie cutter details you have to get used to, but when it comes to options, you are going to have an entire list of things you simply can't expect. These are the things that you have to deal with on a case by case basis.

In other words, when you are working with options, you have to learn how to read as you go. Make case by case decisions and work with that. Yes, there are certain tricks of the trade you need to have under your belt, but overall, you are going to find the best thing to do is make decisions as you go along.

It's going to come easy to you once you get the basics down, trust me.

But while the different types of options are important, that's not all you need to know to get started. Don't worry, next we are going to look at some of the other important details you need to get started in your options trading.

And they are going to get your jump start underway, so in no time at all you are going to be on the options section of the stock market, and rising to the top.

Chapter 4 – The Bears and the Bulls

By now I am sure you are incredibly used to the different lingo that is used on the stock market, no matter what part of the market you are on.

By now, you have to know the basics that you want to gravitate toward, and the other things you want to avoid. I am sure you are getting a real feel for how you should be overall, but the little risks you can take here and there that are going to lead to the greatest profits.

But, what you may not know, is what the terms bear and bull mean, and how you can use these terms to launch your options career even faster and to a greater end.

For starters, it is important to note that both bear and bull markets give incredible opportunities for gaining a lot of profit.

They do this in different ways, and you will, of course, need to find the best way that works for you. Overall, however, these are the markets you want to have sitting in front of you

So let's get started in how you can use both of these markets to your advantage.

The bear market:

First of all, a bear market is a market that has dropped at least twenty percent in the past year. It can, of course, be more than this, but in general, the twenty percent is standard.

This is measured from the closing lows to the closing highs.

But that doesn't mean your profits are going to go out the window. In fact, there are many ways you can make a lot of money in both of these kinds of markets, in spite of the fact they are dropping.

The three most effective things you can do to make a profit in a bear market are simple:

1. **Sell your reserves**

You know you have those stocks that you have been holding on to for times like this? Well the time is here, so sell them!

2. **Exercise your rights as a put holder**

As you know, you have the right with puts to sell at a higher price before the expiration date, even in a market that is dropped. So, if you have a stock that you want a certain amount for, you know the market has dropped, but you want to sell it anyway, you can get the same price you had originally wanted for it... simply because of the kind of option it is.

3. **It's time to look at the short term**

Many investors want those long term investments, always looking for ways to make money in the future. While that is an excellent thing to do as a stock holder, you do have to remember that there are going to be fluctuations in the market, and as such you will be much better off having some short term plans.

Invest in stocks you can sell easily, especially when the market has dropped, or look for various programs that allow you to profit even in the downturns. There are plenty of short term solutions to when this happens, but you have to be willing to go out there and find what they are.

Many investors, especially those that are investing for the first time, tend to panic when they see there is a drop in the market. They think that they are going to enter into a steady spiral, and end up losing all their money.

Of course it can be scary to see the market take a downturn, but rest assured that it always happens, and it will get better, it always does. Your goal is to figure out ways you can keep the profits coming in even when it is on the downward turn.

As with most things on the stock market, there are opposites that happen. When the market is taking a downturn, it is called a bear market, but a bull market, on the other hand, is characterized as when the market rises suddenly

While it may seem like a great thing to happen up front, you do have to still be careful. Not all stocks are going to profit from a sudden upward turn in the market, and there are still ways you can lose money.

But, there are also plenty of ways you can make money, you just have to know how.

Just as there were three things you can do in the bears market to keep the profits coming in, here are three things you can do in a bulls market for the same result.

1. Begin taking on the long term

In other words, do the opposite of buying stocks in anticipation of a rainy day, but rather, buy stocks with the anticipation of the stock prices rising. You can learn how to do this effectively with time and little research.

2. Play the call game

You know what puts and calls are, but until now you have been focusing on the puts. It's time to put yourself in the driver seat and take on the other end of the spectrum... the calls.

3. Keep an eye on the market trades, and plan your next move

Again, go with the long term. When the market is rising, it can become your impulse to sell sell sell and get the most profits you can, but just remember that everything that goes up, is going to come down, and that means you have to again plan for the market downturns.

I don't want to put an attitude of pessimism in you... because you can gain a lot of profits from both kinds of markets, but what I do want to put in you is the attitude that things are going to change.

If they are going great, they are going to start to go down after a while, and if they are going poorly, they are going to start to go up. As tempting as it is, don't ever get stuck thinking that this is it, you have reached the point in the market where it won't change again.

Because it always will.

Chapter 5 – Tips and Tricks of the Trade: Getting Your Own Options Started

I strongly feel the key to success in anything is to have a thorough knowledge of that topic before you dive on in. Yes, there are some variations and exceptions to this in my mind, but generally, you are going to walk away with the best results if you know what you are doing going in.

So until now, I have carefully set up the knowledge of the options side of the market, the things you can expect, the minor details you have to watch out for, and the kinds of markets that are going to give you the best results.

Now, while there are most definitely going to still be learning curves, things you can only learn from experience, and things you need to develop your own preferences on, I think it is time we get you started in your own options trading.

Again, as much as I feel you should know about a topic before you dive into it, I also feel you should take things slow. Of course it would be nice to dive in and get up and going now, but the faster you rush into things, the more likely it is you will make a mistake.

In its most basic form, to get started in your trading, all you need to do is buy a stock, watch what it does, and sell it.

Of course there are a wide range of factors that follow these basic, and with each basic principle you are going to have other things to take into consideration, but for the most part, your trading is going to be relatively the same basic set of events.

Now, when you first get started, I know you are going to have dreams of making it rich, getting more and more stocks and investments while you buy, sell, and trade the ones you already have, and all in all achieve the success you have heard of others achieving.

And you can do it. You can buy, sell, trade and succeed every turn in the road, and you can climb the ladder of Wall Street or the stock market or anywhere else you are dreaming of.

But, I want to do a bit of a reality check now. Before you get settled into your new trading and let all of your dreams and day jobs go, there are a few key points you have to know. They aren't earth shattering, but they are true, and they are going to put your entire investment career into perspective.

Here are the five most important things you have to remember when you are getting started in your stock trading.

They aren't going to guarantee anything, and of course there are exceptions to every rule, but all in all, these are things you need to know to ensure you don't give up right out of the shoot.

1. You will most likely fail in the first year of trading

This is something that is as much experience as it is skill. You can learn the basics, you can do everything absolutely right, and you can dedicate your heart and soul to this, but you are still most likely going to fail in your first year.

That's just the way things are, it isn't an indicator of how well you are going to do in the future, it's just how it happens.

2. **There is no fool proof plan, no completely secure market, and no guarantee that nothing is going to go wrong**

You will find those people that claim to have a 'fix' on the market, and you will find those people that claim they have it all together. You are going to find those people that guarantee they have what it takes to make your rich... and you have to ignore all of it.

Go ahead and try some of the tips and tricks, and go ahead and use what tools they give you, but know that there are still risks to take and ways you can lose... and when it comes to stocks, that can happen quickly.

3. **There are going to be fluctuations in the market... more often than not... no exceptions**

Sure, it would be nice to have a market that was going to stay the same no matter what. One where you knew that things were going to happen a certain way, and where you knew that you could rely on things to turn out another way.

But, that just isn't the way things are. You are going to have to deal with the ups and the downs no matter how good at the market you become, everyone does.

4. **You will make money at this, but you will more than likely not become incredibly rich**

So many people have dreams of becoming the next Warren Buffet, and while there is nothing wrong with dreaming, you have to remember that while you most definitely can make money at this, and even make enough money to support yourself, you are most likely not going to become extremely rich with the stock market.

5. **You will always be losing trades, even if you are at the very top of the game**

Some people get it in their heads that if they are at the game long enough, they are only going to win and never lose, but again, that is just not the case.

There are going to be ups and downs in the market, just like there are going to be rises and falls in your stocks. Sure, you are going to do better at some points, and you are going to do worse at some points, but all in all, there are going to be the ups and downs that you have to deal with just like everyone else.

Now, I don't want to discourage you or make you think that options are too risky, in fact, you can actually make really decent money with them. What I am trying to do is show you that you can make a living at the market, and you are going to succeed, even if you do fail at first.

Many of the issues people have with options trading is the fact they get pessimistic and think that they are losing if they don't make a lot of money at it, especially at first.

What I am trying to show you is that you aren't failing, and you can, in fact, expect a lot of setbacks on the outset of this game. It's only after you stick with it that you begin to see steady success, and even then you have to deal with the ups and downs.

Chapter 6 – Beginner's Luck: How To Avoid Common Mistakes and Stay On Track From the Beginning

We all want to see success at our endeavors right from the beginning. We want to get started, climb to the top, and see it happen. In fact, it would be most ideal to be able to watch the steady increase to the top happen quickly, so you don't have to waste a lot of time waiting for that to happen.

But, that's just not the way things are.

If you are going to rise to your top in the stock market, you are going to have to take the time to get there, and you are going to have to deal with the setbacks and downfalls in the process.

To put it bluntly, every beginner makes mistakes, that is just the way it goes. If you are going to succeed, you have to go through the pitfalls.

There are mistakes that every beginner makes, simply because they are beginners. Here I want to show you some of those mistakes, and help you avoid making them. This, in turn, is going to make your rise go smoothly, and you don't have to deal with as many setbacks as others have.

Mistake number 1. You don't have enough patience

As I already said, you are more than likely to have to stick with this for a year or two before you enjoy any real results. This means you are going to have to deal with twelve months of failure... at least.

Don't give up. If you stick with it, it will pay off.

Mistake number 2. You put too much money into this too soon

The stock market can become a problem if you aren't smart about it, and the more you pump your money into it, the more potential you have to lose that money.

Make sure you invest wisely, and that you always check to ensure you are able to spare the money you put into the market. Never put in any money that you can't afford to lose, even if the market looks secure.

You never know when the market is going to take a downward turn, and you could find yourself penniless in a heartbeat if you don't plan wisely. I don't want to scare you off, I just want to make sure you have the money you need to make it happen.

Mistake number 3. You don't put enough money into this

On the opposite end of the spectrum, you have to use money to make money, and the options are no exception. If you don't have a lot of money to put in, you can expect it to take longer to get the profit out of it.

If you want to start bigger and faster, take a period of time to save up money to invest. Again, don't put in money that you can't afford to lose, so set aside the money first then put it in.

This way, you are going to have enough money to get started, but at the same time you aren't going to risk losing any money that you really need.

Mistake number 4. You give up too soon

You may be thinking right now that a year isn't so bad, but trust me, it can be a lot harder than you think. If you are going to rise to the top of your game, then you really do have to stick with this the amount of time it takes to get there.

I know a whole year is a long time, but at the same time, you have to realize just how long it is. Maybe right now you are thinking that there's no way you could stick with it for so long, and let me encourage you to give it a shot.

On the other hand, maybe you think that you are going to breeze right through. If that's the case, stick with it, because it is going to get hard, and you are going to have to deal with some of the rough times to get to the success you are hoping for.

Mistake number 5. You don't give it a real chance

So many people want to see the results, and the numbers right up front. If you want to do this, you have to give it a real chance. I know what it's like. I've been there, but trust me, the more you stick with it, the easier it is going to be.

You are going to begin to see those numbers go up, and your bank account is going to reflect the change. You are going to see the success you want to see, and you are going to get better at your trading.

For this to happen, however, you have to stick with it in the long run. You have to deal with the ups and downs before you get to the point where you can trade with ease and confidence.

Take each trade, sale, and purchase as a learning experience. Count the progress you make, and learn from the setbacks. The more you put into this, the better off you are going to be overall.

I know it can be hard to be patient, but trust me, a little bit of patience now, or even a lot of patience right now is going to pay off in the long run. So get out there and put in the work that you need.

Time, dedication, and patience are the three things you need on your side now, and you are going to end up with the results you want.

So get out there and invest.

Conclusion

There you have it, everything you need to know about options trading.

Now that you are at the end of the book, I know it seems like a lot less of a big deal. Now you know how you choose the right options for you, you know how to command these options, and you know how to get the most out of your trades.

All in all, you know what you need to do to make the profits come in, and you know how to make choices that give you the results that you want. There's no end to the ways you can use this to your benefit, and the more you practice, the better off you are going to be.

That is my end goal with this book, and that is what I want you to focus on as you make your way through the large world of stocks. There's no end to the ways you can use this to your advantage, and there's no end to the ways you can increase your profits.

The more you know about how all of this works, the better off you are going to be, and the easier things are going to get with later investments. I know there are a lot of questions you still need answered, and I know there are going to be things you have to learn from experience, but my goal with this book was to give you something that you could use with confidence.

Something that was going to show you that you can be the investor you have dreamed of being, and that you don't need to fear the stock market or the things that are in it. There's no end to the ways you can make this work, and the more you use it, the easier it is going to be the next time around.

So if you are tired of the same old stocks ending up in the same old way, then you are in the right place. This book is going to change the way you do your stocks and the way you handle your investments... leading to the better changes you need to make to take care of your profits.

All in all, this is your answer to the world of options trading, giving you another leg up in the stock world.

Now get out there and put what you have learned to the test. You are going to feel on top of the world with the incredible results you see, and you won't ever want to turn back again.

Happy investing.

Made in the USA
Middletown, DE
01 August 2018